ANCHOR BOOKS

HEAD OVER HEELS

Edited by

Rachael Radford

First published in Great Britain in 2003 by
ANCHOR BOOKS
Remus House,
Coltsfoot Drive,
Peterborough, PE2 9JX
Telephone (01733) 898102

HB ISBN 1 84418 142 1
SB ISBN 1 84418 143 X

FOREWORD

Anchor Books is a small press, established in 1992, with the aim of promoting readable poetry to as wide an audience as possible.

We hope to establish an outlet for writers of poetry who may have struggled to see their work in print.

The poems presented here have been selected from many entries, and as always editing proved to be a difficult task.

I trust this selection will delight and please the authors and all those who enjoy reading poetry.

Rachael Radford
Editor

Contents

LOVE SHADOWED US

I did not love you on first meeting.
'Beautiful Dreamer,' you crooned. Like Bing?
Don't laugh. Sly moon was cheating.
Soft breeze swayed the sea to sing.
An accidental touch of finger-tips;
Love shadowed us along the shore.
Precipitated brushing of shy lips
made gentle introduction to a more
impassioned mood. Discreet moon withdrew
behind a passing cloud. Love led our life
through pleasant ways that sometimes went askew.
I love you. Then and now I am your wife.
God took you through the universal gate.
Love stands eternal. Patience bids me wait.

Joan Barnett

Love Is

Love is a gesture, love is a toy
Love is a game between a girl and a boy.

Love is a challenge, love is a duel
Love is a folly that can leave you feeling like a fool.

Love is a banquet, love is a feast
Love can be the beauty or love can be the beast.

Love for some once they have been bitten
Heralds true love, forever smitten.

L E Marchment

YOU'LL BE FINE IN TIME

Leave the past behind you, it's really easy to say.
Live a different life, a different kind of way.
Change your clothes and hair, move to another town,
Take educational classes, wear a smile, not a frown.
Get a different outlook, completely change your life,
You've really had enough of all this trouble and strife.
Words of wisdom spoken, everyone seems to know best,
But what goes on inside my head, never leaves my mind to rest.
I act as though I'm fine, I always seem so well,
The life and soul of the party, you'd never really tell.
Inside my head is shattered, my heart well hardened with time,
But don't ever worry about her, I'm sure she'll be quite fine.
The daily drudge of routine, the time clock tickin' by,
The sun from east to west, sets in a deep red sky.
The time ticks by so quickly, each morning a brand new day,
But still the pain remains, fated with me to stay,
Of a heart stood still in time, of memories faded and grey
For always loving you, a higher price I had to pay.
I never can forget you, they say I will in time,
But time's a tickin' on now, I'm sure I'll be quite fine.

R S Thomas

WHAT IS LOVE?

Love is caring, love is kind
Love is knowing . . . though sometimes blind
Love is sharing, love is abundant!
Love is needed . . . never redundant
Love is selfless, love is patient
Love is giving . . . never complacent
Love is loyal, love is fair
Love is open and sincere
Love is faithful, love is wise
Love is truth, love never lies
Love is tender, love is calm
Love brings peace . . . never harm
Love is hopeful, love endures
Love never fails but perseveres
Love is strength, love will build
In times of weakness love will shield
Love considers, love respects
Love brings comfort and protects
Love is warming, love surrounds
In trust and faith love is found
Love is beauty, love gives light
Love has reason, love unites
Love is fruitful when love unifies
Love brings happiness to all our lives.

Gina Marie Alma

TIME

Time is the great healer
Or so I've heard it said.
And I have to say
That this is true,
Now you're not in my head.

You used to haunt me every day
And all my night-times too.
I never thought
That it would end,
So in love was I with you.

But you cured me of my fantasies
With every tear I cried,
With every hurt
You made me feel,
A part of my love died.

I could not make you love me
In the way that I loved you.
So here I am
Left with no choice,
But to take my heart from you.

And I will keep it safe and warm
And protect it from all pain,
And when I feel
The time is right,
I'll try to love again.

Cari

THE FLAME HAS GONE

Where has the love deep inside of me gone?
I search day after day - but there is none.
I like and admire him, he's my best friend
But where is the love that will help us to mend?

He's the father of my children - whom I adore,
But I no longer have the feelings I had before.
He still makes me smile and still makes me laugh,
He's small, I'm tall - so he calls me a giraffe!

We never hold hands or sit on one another's lap,
We hardly make love or together take a nap.
We rarely hug and kiss like we did before,
It's my fault - I'm to blame, I know.

He comes forward to kiss me, I move away,
I don't know why - but it's the same every day.
He's now growing tired of the rejection I show,
But I don't know how to show my love anymore.

I need him to know I do have feelings inside,
Which are waiting to surface - forever they can't hide.
I am so pre-occupied with so many other things,
That sometimes I don't realise I'm going round in rings.

I promise I will never leave him, we are soul mates I feel,
But I do understand why he now often screams.
I'm a mystery to him and a mystery to me,
I don't understand how to help him to see.

Vicki Watson

Love's Promise

(Inspired by Mam and Judy)

Love once gained is never lost
Through times of trouble and rough seas tossed
Through joys and heartache, illness and good health
Through harder times from dearth to wealth
This love that grows so strong and true
Within our families, within me and you
This love that binds like ropes of steel
Will bring with it the power to heal.
When memories of the happier times come
As you sit in the chair feeling sad and forlorn
Please open your heart, feel that love round about you
Feel comfort in knowing I share those memories too
This love that we shared hasn't disappeared you see
This love is still strong and it's coming from me
Please understand it was my time to go
But I haven't gone far, I'm only next door
Just because you can't see me, don't think I'm not there
I will never leave you, this bond we still share
Be brave my love, though you'll shed many tears
I'll be right there with you through each passing year
I would never leave the ones I love most
So much love once gained is never lost
You'll feel it around you as each new day calls
Until the day that you join me, then you'll understand all.

Marion Drew

FINDING THE RIGHT PARTNER

(Later life)

The children are gone, you are now on your own
With time for each other, a lifetime to share.
Though passion is not of the earlier years,
The warmth and the love will always be there.

The caring and sharing, in so many ways
Will show all the world that your marriage is strong.
A touch or a look that across the years stays,
Forever together, you know you belong.

When the glitz and the glamour have gone from your love
And the heights that you reach are no longer great,
You will *know* you have picked the right partner in life
If they're still by your side, as your friend and your mate.

Tony Fuller

YOU

You occupy my thoughts by night and day
I try to dismiss you
But you return to make me feel so blue
With you life could be so fine
But I know you can never be mine

I try to understand why it has to be this way
And my laughter turns into dismay
Every time I see you my heart dies
But no one can see through my lies

My feelings run so deep
But all I can do is weep
As our story ends
And we part not even as friends.

Varsha Maisuria

The Singer

I knew this singer called Phil
Who could always give me a thrill,
The singer in the pub
Looking good in any club.
Our first kiss was too much,
Stuck together, lonely to touch.
Shame he was married,
Loved his kids so crazy,
We could never lie.
Together we could never make that tie.
He goes away to join a famous group
I believe, what a troupe.
Then again he was playing nearby,
So I went to see him, nearly to cry.
His wife was there too,
I think she did she had a clue,
Not that she would sing on stage
Perhaps this is the end of the page.
Just thinking and dreaming of where
Is he now and what does he share?

Pauline Milman

ADDICTION

I'm addicted to you I can't pull away
Other people don't matter, I hear what you say
But I'm society's creation, it made me like this
And I need some approval beyond prejudice.

Yet your touch and your hold make me feel so good
I want it to work, if only it could.
Your soul draws me near you with such magnetic appeal
How can I listen to them, when I know what I feel?

If I could take us anywhere it wouldn't be here
We'd escape far away where no one could leer.
We'd dance in the sunshine and kiss all day long
With no one to tell us that our togetherness is wrong.

Kim E Breckon

TRUE LOVE?

Was I in love when I was ten?
Fair Bridie Moon as she was then.
A stolen kiss behind a tree,
She taught me dance. Did she love me?

'Dear John,' wrote lovely Mary-Ann,
'I fear I've found another man.
A sailor? Much to long away,
I need a lover here to stay.
I loved you true,' said that dear she,
It ended there for sure for me.

Disillusioned now at twenty-one,
'Til once again I felt the sun.
Breathtaking stars, romantic moon
Enchanting, sparkling, lovely June.
I see her now with eyes of blue,
With changing light a different hue,
A smile attracting such response
Changing dark to light at once.
I swore I'd love her 'til I died,
And then discovered that she'd lied.
Another man she had elsewhere,
She disappeared into thin air.

Calloused heart, insouciant,
For me no other love event.
Women yes, a score perhaps,
But not one did my heart entrap.

I married though and over time
I learned to love sweet Clementine.
She bore me children, strong and fair,
Devoted mother, full of care.

Alas before we settled in
To aged comfort, times serene,
She died and left us crushed with grief,
Aching hearts without relief.

Was I in love when I was ten?
Is love true now? Or was it then?

Cyril Joyce

My Sweet Love

The love we had was sweet and true,
So romantic that no one knew.
The times we had, just me and my guy,
Lips to lips and eye to eye.
The first kiss was the sweetest thing
And no one knew what love can bring.
Strong together, couldn't tear us apart
I was so in love, but he took my heart.
Our relationship he wanted to end
And said he'd rather be my friend.
That night I cried myself to sleep,
But the wound on my heart was much too deep.

Sophie Trenchard

Stand Up And Take A Bow

Everyone needs one good friend
On whom you really can depend.
My best friend is my husband,
Against the world we two stand.

He loves me just the way I am,
Is always there if I get in a jam.
He makes me laugh and smile,
So my life is more worthwhile.

Someone in whom I can confide,
No need my fears or tears to hide,
Was it luck or a quirk of fate
When we met on that blind date?

He said it was love at first sight,
Did I know he was my 'Mr Right'?
We married while still in our prime,
My love grew with the passage of time.

Over the years I learnt to say,
'I love you,' every single day.
Colin, I want to say this now,
Please stand up and take a bow!

Rosemary Davies

YOU ARE MY SUNSHINE

If every day was dreary
If the streets were paved with snow
If it rained down from the heavens
There would always be a glow
If the gentle winds erupted
Into a raging gale
My happiness and laughter
I know would never fail
If the trees were bare of blossom
And leaves lay on the floor
Brown and dry and lifeless
I would never wish for more
And if summer never showed her face
If she never came to bare
Her warming rays upon me
I know I would not care
For every day you're near me
For every time you call
For every time you touch me
I feel that I may fall
Deeper in love with you
My heart begins to race
At any given moment
In any time or place
Your love is like the sunshine
That brightens up my life
And to share within your sparkle
I would gladly sacrifice.

Carla Marie Haynes

THE LIGHTNING STRIKE

Time arcs across the room, each time I look at you
Like chain lightning, striking from a distance of a mile or two.
A sharp intense flash of blinding light as it punishes the ground.
A millisecond of pure beauty, yet void of any sound.
From within the earth the cacophony inevitably follows, slowly at first
A rumbling crescendo that threatens to make my ears burst,
A tremor so low that the floor gently starts to sway.
It runs through my body, buckling it forward as if to pray,
To this awe-inspiring sight held in my golden eyes,
That reflects this vignette, so close my body desperately tries
To reach out unafraid and take your hand in mine.
Restricted and restrained, I am motionless without time,
Lost in silence, and the serenity it eventually brings,
You stand alone a sentinel statue, unfolding your wings,
And the rush of cold air that spreads as they are unfurled,
Marks the boundary I have breached to exist in your world,
A place where men with no fear in their heart wish to tread,
And follow in the footsteps, somehow intrinsically lead,
Into a moment of pure stillness, a time-lapse delay,
And the sacrifice of my mind seems such a small price to pay.
My eyes start to leaden into an infinite blink,
As I pray that you will still be there
When they open, the lids start to sink,
And start their journey to obscure you from within my mind,
The darkness takes over and the pain gradually subsides.
I am lost once more, a shepherd with no flock to tend,
Drowning in the unforgiving beauty of darkness, I slowly blend
Back in time, before any notion of you existed within me,
I am bathed in the lightning that answered my plea,
As the blinding light recedes you are gone, a void apart,
Yet your vision is burnished forever upon my heart.

Garon Coles

ECHOES

Your eyes flash and a smile lights up your face
And echoes from the past ignite a flame,
A flame that once burned strongly then became
So dim it disappeared without a trace;
Your voice, your laugh are echoes that embrace
Someone who through the years was just a name;
So diff'rent now but somehow still the same
As in that other time, that other place.

And through the echoes mem'ries reassure:
Your face though lined with age is still as fair,
You speak my name as gently as before;
The flame grows strong, new promises are there,
Not echoes but a love that lives once more,
For through those shining eyes your soul you bare.

Hilary J Cairns

For You

My love for you
Is so true.
You're the one for me,
Baby, can't you see?
I want you by my side,
Every day and every night,
We've always been so close.
Every time you're near me,
I can imagine us together,
Now does it have to be
Now you're not near me.
I still feel you close to my heart.

Kirsty Marie Wing

Lot's Wife

If I could be in the Promised Land,
I'd simply stand, and stand, and stand,
Gazing at the boy I loved
When both of us were very young.

All I have is just a few
Mem'ries when my hand held you
In greeting, meeting, so rare, so new
The fleeting moment and not so bold,
I raised my eyes, yours were not cold.

If I could once again be held,
I'd be in the Promised Land and well,
I'd simply stand, and stand, and stand.

Gerasim

Love

Oh heavens above
I think I'm in love
The bait has been bitten
And I've become smitten

My heart gives a tug
At the thought of the bug
For I have been caught
The battle well fought

My heart I shall carry
For my love I'll not tarry
He is the one
My life has begun

For I shall discover
A friend and a lover
A person to mate
For that is my fate.

Emma Gascoyne

My Adonis

There stood my Adonis, oozing with love.
My living angel, sent from above!
I was his Venus, obsessed with his frame!
Every moment breathing his name!

Sun-kissed hair adorning blue, limpid pools,
One look worth more than a thousand jewels!
A twitch of the mouth and a cheeky grin,
A raging fire burning from within!

Cupid's arrow hits target from the start,
Two bodies but one beat of the heart.
He is my true north and I am his south,
Beckoning for the touch of his mouth.

His magnetic field pulling me to him,
Longing for the touch of his skin.
Drunken and senseless by fiery passion,
May these feelings continue in fashion.

Immortal love binds two cords into three,
My soul mate for all eternity.
Living for the moment to see his face,
The haven of his soothing embrace.

The feel of his hair; the love in his eyes,
This has to be the ultimate prize.
Unrestrained devotion to only him,
Complete commitment, not just a whim!

My Adonis has not the slightest fault,
Our love is perfect and will not halt.
Butterflies fluttering softly inside,
I'll walk beside him forever with pride!

Val Spall

TRUE LOVE

How couples can be married
For so long, I'll never know.
Couples that stay married for fifty years,
Their love just seems to grow.
What is it about these couples
That stick through thick and thin,
Have they ever thought of being unfaithful,
Or any other kind of sin?
I suppose that's why they last so long,
True love never dies,
True love means you stay with one,
Never having to tell them lies.

S P Hibbeler

A Funny Way To Meet

I'm running late
A voice calls, 'Wait!'
I hear the sound
I spin around
I feel a thud
I see the blood
Through the haze
I see your face
In a casualty bed
With aching head
Feeling tender
I begin to remember
Above the noise
I hear your voice
'Watch my ladder!'
Then I heard the clatter
A lovely bouquet
Arrived that day
The card I read
Here's what it said
'As you fell at my feet
Would you care to meet?
Perhaps it was fate
I'm asking this date?'
The card's now tattered
But that doesn't matter
It's forty years today
That we met that day
What a funny way to meet
Falling at your feet.

Babs M Ward-Schmitz

TOUCHED BY ANGELS

Everything she touches turns to gold
For her love, my heart is sold
The only thing is, she doesn't know
She is Heaven to see, Heaven to behold

She puts rainbows in my heart
And fires, in the deepest parts
She must've been touched by angels
'Cause she brings out the Devil in me

I want her, I need her even more
And these feelings are driving me crazy,
They just tear me apart, rip me up
I feel such emptiness in my heart

She doesn't even know I exist
Anyway! What would a girl like that
Want with a man like me?
What could she possibly see in me?

And I don't want her for just one time
I don't want her for just a good time
I want her for all times
I want her to be mine, all the time

She must've been touched by angels
I want her, I need her even more
She's Heaven to see, Heaven to be near
And I don't want her for just a good time. Hell no!

David McDonald

MY LOVE

My love is like the deep blue sea,
It can be calm or rough.
There are hidden depths for you and me,
Which are both soft and tough.

My love is like the endless sky,
It can be dark or light,
There's such variety for you or I
Which may be dull or bright.

My love is like the days and years,
They can be happy or sad,
There are many shared hopes and fears
Which are both good and bad.

My love is like the moon and stars,
They can be hidden or seen,
There's a bond surviving many wars
Which is both strong and serene.

My love is like this life of ours,
It can be short or long.
There are weaknesses, but also powers,
Which keep us firm and strong.

S J Dodwell

AN ANGEL IN YOUR POCKET

I'll put an angel in your pocket
To drive away the night,
I'll put an angel in your pocket
To make everything all right.

I'll put an angel in your pocket
To chase away your fears,
I'll put an angel in your pocket
To dry up all your tears.

I'll put an angel in your pocket
To keep all ills at bay,
I'll put an angel in your pocket
To brighten up each day.

I'll put an angel in your pocket
To keep watch over you,
I'll put an angel in your pocket
To show my love is true.

I'll put an angel in your pocket,
I have just one to spare,
For you are my angel in my pocket,
I hope you always will be there.

S M Hooper

LINDA

I wish I'd never loved you, I wish we had never met.
That beautiful October day now fills me with regret.
If only I'd never loved you and didn't love you still,
I wouldn't be on life support, I wouldn't be so ill.

I wish I'd never trusted you to care for my tender heart,
Those danger signs that warned me, I should have seen them from the start.
If only I hadn't believed you when you gave me all those lies,
About your love being as eternal as the starlight in the skies.

I wish I hadn't opened up my heart and soul to you,
When you promised everlasting love, a love so deep and true.
If only I hadn't trusted you with the key into my life,
I wouldn't be lying here now, a victim of this knife.

Terry Traynor

THE KISS SONNET

Your kiss is very deadly,
With a flavour all its own,
Your lips glow very redly,
It's a most erotic zone:
Your tongue seeks mine and finds it
And deftly they entwine.
Your love ties bonds around my heart and binds it,
Your kiss has much more sweetness by far than wine.
When cupid fired his dart at me,
My heart he couldn't miss,
The wound he made is deeper now
That I've tasted your kiss:
Your kiss is quite sufficient to fill me with desire,
Your love ignites my very heart and sets my soul on fire.

Mick Nash

Love Lives In Another Place

(Dedicated to Faye)

In the stillness of our own space
Our friendship and love
We'll for ever embrace.

Whenever your dad visits your place,
There's a knowing, restful smile,
He puts on your face.

He brings peace and spiritual fulfilment
To me and you

Because he knows our hard times too
And how much I care and love you.

Our love for each other
Has taught us expression
And we've both learned
Some valuable lessons

Deep in our souls, we'll never be parted,
Even when we feel broken-hearted.

So whenever I think of you
And tears begin to fill my eyes

My true feelings I will never deny,
For now I know for sure -

No lesser man am I
Whenever I break down and cry.

Graham Hare

Why?

We had that perfect moment,
Many moonlit nights ago.
We had that perfect day,
Since then, my heart beats slow.

I think of what might have been,
I think of what we could have seen.
You were my sun,
You're still shining,
I wish that you could still be mine.

You engraved my heart with 'love you forever.'
I still do, but you never.
I close my eyes and you are near,
But I wish you were here.

As I sleep on the moonlit night,
I see your face, I see the light.
We never did grow old together,
But at heart we're now forever . . .

Nigel James Guy

OFFSHORE SADNESS

Between us may be miles of sea,
Wild oceans keeping us apart,
For those long weeks you are away,
You're only sleeping in my heart.

Few words are spoken before you leave,
A glance and then a smile,
Our last embrace that bit tighter,
Knowing it's to last a while.

Stranded in a stormy sea,
I wait upon the shore,
Counting down the nights and days
Till you walk through the door.

It's the same wind that blows our hair,
The same sun that kisses our skin,
We only have to imagine,
The small world we live in.

My brave, sweet man,
I miss you so,
It only gets harder
Each time you go.

Mandy Keay

Love 2

Love! A simple ; four-lettered word,
Yet to every person ; holds differing meanings,
Being a multi-facet ; contorting, emotion,
Effecting onto each ; in total compulsion,
Yet often - so diverse ; all consuming.

Love of kin and family ; all protecting,
Love of spouse and kids ; completely embracing,
Love of life, fun and joy ; always sharing,
Love of acceptance ; without tracing.

Love of animal, cat or dog ; who's totally loyal,
Love of a car or house ;we're completely declared,
Love of work, being needed ; with dedication,
Love of the good life ; and want to be shared.

Gary J Finlay

Don't You Know?

Don't you know, how much I love you?
Even though, I show I care.
Deep inside my heart is breaking,
For your love I cannot share.

Don't you know, my nights are sleepless?
Yearning for you, in my arms.
Needing your caress and kisses,
Compelling feelings to stay calm.

Don't you know, I love to feel you?
Touching bodies, skin to skin.
Can't you sense my pulse that's racing,
Knowing that I cannot win.

Don't you know, my life is your life?
To direct, as you instruct.
Maybe you'll wake up one morning,
Having realised what you've got.

Sharon Spencer

A LOVER'S PLIGHT

In this broadland, woodland part,
Walks my rose, whence leaps my heart.
My rose, my rose, beguiling me,
Your ev'ry turn so heavenly.
I see thee almost day by day,
Upon your lawn without delay,
When the sun begins to rise,
Walk amid the butterflies.
You are my rose, my dearest one,
Could but my love shine as the sun.
Could but my love be at your feet
As buttercup and meadowsweet.
My rose, your wavy hair, your laughing eyes,
Your fresh complexion, your look - surprise
At a rabbit, darting from out the hedge,
Oh, if only thou couldst hear my pledge.
Oh my misery, if I who withhold,
Could free my springing passion bold.
If only I could ease mine aching breast
And pluck thee with a tender hest.
My rose, my rose, I love thee so,
My drunkenness filled to overflow.
Do not go thither, yet stay awhile -
And look this way at me, and smile.

D Haskett-Jones

44 Years On

Can you look back to fifty-eight,
Waiting for the taxi at your gate?
The sausage roll car brought you to me;
A vision in white for me to see.

You said the words I knew were true.
You belonged to me and I to you.
Not only did our friends hear us,
But God above was blessing us!

It seems to me after these years
Full of laughter, joy and tears,
That the vows we made on that day,
Both of us could still them say.

Now in retirement, at our ease,
I can't get down upon my knees,
But God will hear me when I say,
'Thank you my God each single day.'

I'm not often serious - as you know,
I'm the joker of the pack - that's so,
But when I think back through the years,
My eyes often fill with grateful tears.

Yes! Tears of joy, my darling girl.
I wish I had a flag to unfurl
To tell the world my love for you;
You know I love you through and through.

So as we celebrate once again,
We can eliminate the pain
And with hearts filled with joy and love,
Thank our Lord in Heaven above.

My sweetheart, please accept this verse,
It may for us have been much worse,
But as it turned for us both,
I'm glad we both plighted our troth.

Tony Olivey

MISSING YOU

Missing you is rather funny
For now you are not there,
Yet every day I look for you
Every everywhere.

Missing you is rather funny,
For you are not there when I shout,
But then I remember you have gone,
Of that there is no doubt.

Missing you is rather funny,
I keep expecting to see you,
But where, just where upon this Earth,
Where are you living like you do?

Keith L Powell

LORNA

The years slip by.
You never lose that smile,
That knot we tied
Has never been broken.
That's love put to the test,
Which makes you the best.

David Bruce Moffatt

CARER'S HONEST LOVE

In many homes throughout the land,
A life is lived, that wasn't planned.
Where people hold their own, alone,
A love no longer even known.
Where once was love there lies a void,
But honour keeps them still employed.
The person that they once held dear,
Lives now alone in days of fear.
And yet the love that once was warm,
Is keeping them still safe from harm.
As outside normal days slip by,
You're working hard and wonder why?
But memory keeps ever bright,
Those blessed days and warmer nights.
Until the day you lose the need,
Your life is one more kindly deed.

H E Clarke

LOVE

The moon is full and so to speak,
My being is so too.
From the slumber I do creak
And crane my head for you.

Rise this body from its rest,
Chase away the ghost,
Seek what life can give to me,
But look for you the most.

So it rears right up to strike
And drink the holy wine,
Give all of love back to you
In all of Heaven's time.

Something going on in my brain,
A message for only me,
Strange feeling, very strange,
Can't hide but only see.

Like a fire here in my head,
Flames fanned by the years,
Started by all the good times,
Quenched by all the tears.

C Bramley

SWEET YESTERDAY

I miss you just as much today
As when you first were called away
And went to your eternal home,
Leaving me feeling bereft, alonc.

I miss your presence all the while,
Your voice, your touch, your special smile.
Though memories keep you near me still,
Nothing the aching void can fill.

And since you left this vale of tears,
Throughout the passing of the years,
I love you just as much today
As in the past sweet yesterday.

Edith Stell

BELOVED

I'll never find what I require,
A loving beauty that I desire.
You were sent by the Lord above
And I do believe for me to love.
He plucked you out from all the rest,
For he knew I'd love you best.
A throbbing heart that you have won,
Take care of it, as I have done.
When I go to Heaven and be afar,
I'll paint your name on every star
So that the angels will know and see
Beloved, what you mean to me.
If you're not there by judgement day,
I'll know you've gone the other way,
So I will give the angels back each wing,
The golden harp and everything.
It's just to show you what I'll do,
I'd go through hell to be with you.

J R H Graham

My Love

As I walked slowly to the altar,
I walked with steps that did not falter,
I made a vow to be his wife
And truly love him all my life.
That vow was not too hard to keep,
We rarely had a row.
At times of course, we begged to differ,
It often happens when you have a little nipper.

Lots of laughter, not many tears,
We had so many happy years.
Then he went, and I was on my own,
Down here on Earth and so alone.
But still I know, I'll feel his spirit land,
And take me gently by the hand.
No need to think of earthly things,
He'll fit me with a pair of wings.

Constance E Bush

My Only Love!

Only eight when she smiled at me,
Oh, how fast my heart did beat
And a trembling of the knee,
I ask, 'What is happening to me?'

This love that I had was mine alone,
That no one else could share,
So sweet and divine, so utterly mine,
From youth to aged, this love sublime!

I realised as the years went by
I was snared like a spider with a fly!
Caught and trapped, cared not I,
Only if I should lose her!

Now that I have, to the Lord above,
Who has taken to Him my only love,
A lifetime of love she gave to me,
To last and to keep for eternity!

And I loved her so!

W E Clements

My Love

Now love is a treasure
We keep in our hearts,
Of wonderful dreams
From which we won't part.

We've nursed them,
We've cursed them
When they wouldn't come true;
Then suddenly they did,
Right out of the blue.

Those treasures were never
The 'jewels' of life,
Just being together
As husband and wife.

We didn't need gold coins -
No silver or furs -
Just being together
As him and her.

Beth Spinks

My Love . . .

Sometimes I sit and wonder
If you miss me when I'm gone,
And then I sit and ponder
All the things that I've done wrong.

So many times I tried and tried
To tell you how I feel.
Deep inside, I would have died
If your true love wasn't real.

All the times I've sat and cried,
My tears of sorrow true,
Always there right by my side,
No one loves me like you do.

As your soft hand wipes a tear
From my face, I quiver,
The warmth your touch gives so dear,
I know your love's forever.

Marion McGarrigle

DREAMS

As we sleep side by side on our pillows
Gently dreaming the night-time away
In a magical world where our dreams are unfurled
We wait the return of the day.

We don't know where we go when we're dreaming
Laying snug cuddled up in our beds
Or if there's a meaning or reason
For the visions we see in our heads.

Our minds are set free as we slumber
Free to roam this dreamland at its will
To meet family and friends who no longer exist
And meet those who remain with us still.

Not all dreams that we dream make us happy.
There are times when our dreams can be sad.
We may dream of a loved one whose loss broke our hearts,
Like a mother, a sister, a dad.

Would be nice if we both dreamed together
Both were part of the very same dream
We could walk hand in hand through this fantasy land
And see all the strange sights to be seen.

All too soon day returns and it's morning
All our dreams disappear with the dawn
Once again we are back in this everyday world
We sit up, rub our eyes and we yawn.

D Parkes

The Last Thing I Expected

The last thing I expected, when I was packing my case
Was to go on holiday to Kavos and see your happy face.

At first I wasn't sure, so I tried to play it cool
But before I knew what was happening
I was acting like a love-sick fool.

You spun my world around, what was I to do?
My heart was beating faster
Because of this Italian I hardly knew.

The language was a problem
But it didn't stop us from getting along
I knew there was something special about you
There wasn't anything that made it feel wrong.

We spent more time together
I felt relaxed, content and secure
But I told myself it must come to an end
Holiday romances never last for sure.

We went our separate ways
But you'd knocked me off my feet
As soon as you left, I felt lost and alone
With you everything was, well just so neat.

The last thing I expected when we said goodbye
Was that this would last forever
But I'm not going to question why.

Because when you find someone to love
Wherever they live on this Earth
You'll find your own way to make it work
If you hold on to it for all its worth.

Tamzin Hardy

TRANSIENT ROMANCE

love at first sight
on the verge of night
roaming through the dark
in a silent park
silly laughter flight
bright streets at midnight
quick tumultuous love
behind a dark window above
a couple of fine days
illusive honey haze
after all that bliss
something went amiss
regrets are in vain
nothing will remain
but this melancholy glance
on a transient romance . . .

Brigitte Müller

Dear Departed

Will you remember me when
Day is done and night draws on?
When the car won't start,
To whom will you run?
When life is dull, how will you have fun?

When the house needs painting,
The lawns want cutting
And the gardens want digging,
Who will you choose to do your bidding?

Will you call when you need a hand
To walk from the beach - with shoes full of sand,
The bags and the shoes, wet towels as well,
Who will give help to a girl like you?
I would - if I could still be there to give you my hand.

Malcolm Myhill

THIS TIME

(Dedicated to Eddie)

It's silent as you sleep tonight
The raindrops reflect from the street light
Something inside touches my heart
You brought back the girl that fell apart
Everything's peaceful as you sleep
The stars are hidden like the feelings I keep
You hold the key to my love inside
But yet still this heart has a feeling to hide
A feeling of happiness, a secret smile
The extra bit of love that makes it all worthwhile.
Gently I place you a loving kiss
Nothing has ever touched me like this
Never feeling this way before
I cry the tears to beg for more
You're my heart, my true everything
I treasure every bit of love you bring
Can't hide the way I feel, love grows strong
My heart, spirit and mind to you they belong
Holding you in my arms I come to realise
This love can't be hidden, it's placed in my eyes
Each time I look at you I see
Perfection, this time it's true to me
You're so special in every way
I'll hold on forever and never stray
Still in silence, the raindrops fall
The stars appear with my call
Right out to your heart from mine
A wish to feel this way for you throughout time
To keep that extra beat inside this heart
And treasure our memories and never part
I now realise that you're the one
There's no more love to hide, the fears are gone
Then you wake, I've been placed a heart of new
Knowing this time . . . God gave me you.

Janine Williams

Sheila

(April 15th 2002, aged 68)

Some wrinkles now where once were none,
Her hair has turned to grey,
But still that smile, with hint of fun
Remains to make my day.
Those bold brown eyes still gladly show
Her love for me - with this they glow.

Few people's love can last this long;
I'm blessed without a doubt.
My love for her is just as strong,
It's always been throughout.
Our love was always meant to last
And go beyond when we are past.

To me she's still that lovely girl
I married long ago.
She still can put me in a whirl
With just a glance, I know.
It's marvellous, beyond my ken,
For I'm the luckiest of men.

Jax Burgess

THE ETERNAL TRIANGLE

There are two men in my life,
Some say this cannot be true,
But my feelings for this other man
Over several years just grew.
He needed me so very much
And I had love to give,
I felt that I could share my love,
I learned this way to live.
You both have special meaning,
So different in your ways,
You both brought me such happiness
To brighten up my days.
A husband has a special place,
You have taken half my heart,
No need for green-eyed jealousy,
My son has claimed the other half.

S A Clough

SHE

She, is a lady I'm proud to know,
She is a lady of poise and charm,
With a tender heart and her winsome smile
She holds me in her palm.

Her smile is there for everyone,
Her laugh is like a tinkling bell
As it echoes and ripples around the room
And it suits her style so well.

And as she moves around the town
A beauty to behold!
Many eyes will glance her way
With wistful thoughts untold.

That look upon her lovely face
Is a delight for all to see
And one day, maybe, she will turn and beckon,
With a smile, that is just for me!

Bah Kaffir

My Love

If thou shouldst fall from grace,
I'd catch thee in a bed of down -
So soft my warm embrace,
And wipe the spreckled tears that frown
Upon thy lovely face.

I'd cradle thee and would not move,
Save to comfort and impart
All that in me is there by love -
My aching-aching-aching heart.

If thou shouldst phoenix-like arise,
Then vanish in a mist divine,
I'd know that I had lost the prize
And bowing courteously, decline.

James Reeve

Dinner For Two?

A candlelit table,
With crystal and lace,
A single red rosebud
You laid in my place.

Your favourite dinner,
My favourite wine,
Our hands on the table,
Your fingers touch mine.

Low cut and red velvet,
'Our' favourite dress,
your eyes show your thoughts,
I have no need to guess.

As I'm breathing you watch
As my breasts fall and rise,
While my heart pounds within
I can see in your eyes.

That this meal, half forgot now,
Is only the start
Of a long night of love,
You are stealing my heart.

Adrienne

My Deepening Love

My love for you deepens, day by day,
You always call to see me, but then you go away.
I want you, need you, please do stay,
Don't just call then be on your way.

I'm sure you want to settle here
Instead of dashing here and there.
Your mind must be in such a dither,
Running, running, hither and thither.

I cannot bear to see you hurt,
Trampled on, as though you're dirt.
Someone always wanting something,
You give it to them, you have nothing.

Your life is work, work, work,
Always there, you do not shirk.
They're always wanting much more action,
Is there never any satisfaction?

When you have given all you can,
Don't they know you're just one man,
Wanting, taking, no more thanks,
Are you filling all their banks?

You deserve so much pleasure,
Stay with me, enjoy your leisure.
Your life with me could be a dream,
So much happier than it's been!

My love alone will guide you through
All the rough patches life will show,
To let you know your hearth and home
Are here, with me, all that I own.

I will not leave you standing there,
I want you for my love and heir.
If you could give your love to me,
All this I have, would be for thee.

John L Pierrepont

REAL LOVE

A gentle squeeze, fingers entwined
I walk along so proud you're mine
You look so handsome as we walk
Your eyes on mine, no need to talk

Falling in love each stage divine
From our first meeting, drinking wine
We met at friends, you came to chat
And something happened I know that.

We said we'd meet another time
And when we did, it was sublime
Our first embrace, I smell your skin
Then kissing started to begin.

That moment now etched in my brain
I know I'll never be the same
You came and entered in my life
My real dream now to be your wife.

Your hand now letting go of mine
You draw me close, I know this sign
Our lips now meet, a gentle kiss
This is real love no one should miss.

Paula Ely

Facets Of Love

Love is the outpouring of the spirit
In the caring of another's life
The caress of a husband or a wife
The bouncing of a baby on one's knee
Or of feelings just sisterly

Love is service for another
Companionship of a brother
Love is mending a small child's knee
Lovers walking beneath the trees
Love is understanding all of these

Love listens to the unburdening soul
Reaching for life's long goals
Thoughts of the heart life is love
And love is never alone.

Anne Marshall

My Love Poem

As I sit on my bed I think of you
I try to remember just what to do.

To feel you close and holding me tight
Keeping me safe throughout the night

Whether or not you are near or far
You're still not close enough to bar

My feelings of wanting you close to me
So that in your eyes your love I see

That loving look I can't forget
Which I hope will be forever kept.

For me to feel how great that love
We share together, my gentle dove

Come fly me to your arms once more
And take me to another shore

When I feel those gentle arms
And hear once more those loving psalms

Your voice is like a soft caress
Soothing my tensions from my breast

I need to feel your tender kiss
Which I can never, ever resist

The warmth of your lips can melt me so
And will always make sure I never go

Your love for me and mine for you
Will always be forever true

Our love is so deep it is painful to feel
But God is good and will certainly heal

Leaving us deep in each other's arms
With feelings of joy and peaceful calm

Nothing can break two hearts that are one
Anywhere or everywhere under the sun.

Thelma A Oliver

WET AND DRY

Love is like water, splashing about,
Sometimes in and sometimes out.
A few drops are magic and cure many ills,
A whole lot can drown you and like water, kills.

We all have it splashing around in our brain,
I'm sorry that mine is overflowing again.
It's something that suddenly happens to me,
Like the wind and the sun affecting the sea.

You have this attraction like bees to the flowers,
It's such a pity that nothing is 'ours'
So throw me some drops before I die,
Sometimes life is so terribly dry . . .

David Mead

REQUIEM FOR REPOSE

I close my eyes and see
Tears gently rolling on her cheek.
Sweet voice calls urgently to me,
I find I cannot speak!
Now I am back on shingle beach,
Smelling salt from wind-whipped surf.
Multicoloured sea birds strut
Across the bay on lush, green turf.
Parks and gardens where we walked,
Ancient castles we explored,
All the things we talked about
But then, could ill afford!
Those days we spent together
I recollect with ease,
Happiness surrounded us
So easy then, to please.
Now once again, the shadows
Cast around us all by night,
A brief respite from heartache,
Never-ending, such sad plight!
So sleep, so always welcome,
Helps alleviate the pain
That only death can terminate,
To guarantee me sane!

T G Bloodworth

MY LOVE - MY LIFE

You are the sunshine in my day,
The moon and stars at night.
You're the light that shows my way,
You make the wrong things right.
You are the beating of my heart
And every breath I take,
You are the sparkle in my life,
My happiness you make.
You are the answer to my prayers,
My hopes, my dreams and wishes.
You comfort and protect me
With your warm embrace and kisses.
You are my guardian angel,
Sent down from Heaven above,
You are my life and meaning,
My existence is your love.

S Brown

SEPARATION

Though separated we may be
By barriers of time and space,
Our real, essential selves can reach
Across the distance, each to each
And meet in love's embrace.

My soul within me lifts its voice
To pray whatever gods there be
In earth or sky, in Heaven or Hell,
To hold you safe and guide you well
Till you return to me.

Though you may be so far away,
My heart will hear you when you call;
Our lives are joined where dreams unfold,
Where souls can meet and touch and hold
And love is all in all.

We fear no height, we fear no depth,
We fear no powers of earth or sea;
Our love shall stand, though worlds may die,
As constant as the stars on high,
Throughout eternity.

Peter English

KATERYNA

My wife so beautiful and so smart,
In life gives all of her heart.
She cares for all old and young,
With compassion for every one.

In my life she is so supportive,
Giving me help and aid that I can live
She would never knowingly do you a bad turn,
Only be kind, loving and warm.

She's a wonderful mother and fantastic wife,
Being good counsel in my troubled life.
Darling Kateryna is so bright and clever,
I, Richard, will love you forever and ever.

Richard Mazelan

My Love - For Jennifer

When, then - I saw, you,
    In the door of mine heart:
Your gentle, loveliness that flew
    And yet, you're here at the start -
And for you, I'll do the best I can do
    And you'll know, ne'er to depart . . .

Oh lady so kind - such mystery
    In the beauty I beheld
Then. And now as the scene, sees thee
    In the places I held
Your tenderness to me
    And yet, it never gelled . . .

In the sense my love was strange
    To you Jennifer, oh love!
If I could re-arrange
    The history of mine; the 'shove'
That tried t'change
    And yet I remain, yours - love! Dear love!

A N Other

My Love

I search a crowded room to catch a glimpse of him,
His warm returning glance; the very light of him.
His tender hand in mine transmits the love in him.
My heart within me swells; thc very touch of him.

We walk the woodlands ways; love's infinite delights,
Share the deep and dreamless sleep, endless velvet nights.
We fly together on Pegasus - wingèd horse,
Then drown again in Hellespont's turbulent course.

I feel the smooth, soft moistness of his skin,
The steady beat of his dear heart within.
In languorous circles of his love I lie,
Suspended in Elysium 'twixt earth and sky.

Those who knew not hunger, cold and thirst,
Those who knew *not* such deprivation,
We who knew a deep despair and sorrow first,
Could we have such a deep appreciation
Of all life's treasured gifts?

He spends long hours learning Greek to speak,
Because he wants to be with me,
Toils hot days, a pile of stones to seek,
Because he wants to walk with me.

Listening to his snores, long hours I lie awake,
Because I want to lie with him.
His highs and his lows with stoicism take,
Because I want to live with him.

Who, but he, would know just how to please me?
Who, but he, would be allowed to tease me?
Who could succeed, but he, to drive me to distraction,
Partaking so liberally of liquid benediction?

Pam Kearsley

True Love 1941

My whipping-machine was broken
And you came to do the repair,
Up 'til then we had never spoken,
But I really admired your dark hair.
Shyly you smiled and said, 'You're a peach,'
And of course I glowed with pleasure,
The spark was there, within my reach
As we took each other's measure.
On Sundays we would walk beneath
The hills and trees near home,
Of daisy chains you'd make a wreath
As through the sunlit fields we'd roam.
Your arm fit snugly round my waist
As down the country lanes we strolled,
Wild blackberries were ours to taste
And the sun warmed our hearts with gold.
How well I remember our first kiss
Beneath the oak tree's dappled shade,
What unadulterated bliss
Saw our love blossom in that glade.
The back row of the picture house,
It was where you proposed to me,
I was wearing my best pink blouse,
I'd guessed what was coming, you see.
The groom was in naval uniform
And the bride, she of course wore white
And if you'd like to know the form,
This really was love at first sight.

Joan Fletcher

IF I LEAVE SUDDENLY

Please don't worry about the words you didn't say
I know them all
I know them all

Please don't think of the tunes you failed to play
I hear them all
I hear them all

Please don't say I cannot see you grieve
I see it all
I see it all

And most of all don't worry - you never spoke the words
I love you - all
I love you - all

Lift up your heart, reclaim the light
Pass me your burdens in the night
Though I am here and you are there

I know you cared
I know you cared.

Hazel B Cameron

I Want To Be With My Baby

I want to be with my baby
She is my sweetness and my light
I want her . . . and that's not maybe
To consume me both through the day and through the night

I want to be with my baby
We're so close it hurts . . . but that hurt feels right
I want her every day you see
I want my baby with all my might

I want to be with my baby
She is the apple of my eye
So what will be will be
And one day together we will lie

I want to be with my baby
So listen to this please
I can't be without her . . . honestly
My baby's so important to me

So you ask my baby the question
And I'm sure she would agree
Take a walk in my direction
Cos my baby wants to be with me too you see!

Lynn Thompson

My Love

We came into each other's lives when emotionally we were in pain.
Loss we had suffered and felt there was nothing left to gain.
A visit to an ancient city a memory which will always remain.
We walked, talked and warmed to each other,
The day was bright, the air cold and clear,
Suddenly we both knew there was nothing we had to fear.
We viewed the museums in York, the Minster too,
It seemed that now everything was clear.
We departed, climbed onto our coach -
Returning to our homes, to what we realised was a new beginning.
At last, at last, we thought together, we might be winning,
We savoured each other as lovers will.
The ecstasy, the joy, we did and could not stop until we had had our fill.
We tied the knot and pledged our faith,
Seven years have passed since that memorable day.
Together we now are as one, each of us needing the other.
Our love is still strong, though we are older and wiser,
We will and can endure the trials of life,
After all, are we not man and wife?

C Kemper

My Love

Did I ever tell you my love how I feel,
I will put my pen to paper to reveal.

Through all the passing years my love still true,
As I am still very much in love with you,
Sometimes I hear you cry, I feel your pain.
I see your tears like falling rain.

I reach out to hold you tight,
You are the love of my life,
When you are weak, I'll be strong,
Beside you I stand when things go wrong.

Whatever life to us may bring,
My love for you still blooms just like the flowers in spring.
In sickness and in health till death us do part,
My love for you is engraved in my heart.

Ann Marie Millard

My Love

My love is a sort of 'everyday love,'
I don't think it was made by angels above.
My love has been worked at over long years,
Through many a heartache and a soupçon of tears.

It has occasionally faltered, fallen by the way,
But back it comes surging, to fill up my day.
There are no easy marriages, there never could be.
We all want our own way, each one, you and me.

But, my 'everyday love' has survived o'er the years,
And I'm still here loving, combating our fears
Of the Grim Reaper and all that portends.
'Everyday loving' can make you good friends!

Joyce M Jones

LOVE IS . . .

Love is such a little word
And yet it means so much.
It can be given in a silent smile -
Or a fleeting, gentle touch.

It can be shown in so many ways,
Just a helping hand will do,
Or a listening ear, when needed
Let the tenderness shine through.

Love is thinking of others,
And reaching out to give,
An emotion which helps us on our way
In the lives we have to live.

When one loves, it shines around us
And helps us carry on.
So live your life in love's soft light -
It will live on when life is done.

Peggy Hemmings

LONELY LOVE

Love doesn't belong all by itself
Left alone upon a lonely shelf,
It needs warmth, someone to hold,
Not locked away in the bitter cold.

Love needs to be free, left to roam,
Take it with you, give it a home.
Introduce your love so they may rejoice,
Speaking love's words in one united voice!

Don't leave that love all by itself
Or it may remain on its lonely shelf,
With no one to have, no one to hold,
Living in loneliness, bitterly cold.

Colin Devlin

TIDES OF LOVE

Love is like the seashore
Ripple of water over the sand
I love to walk with my love
Holding each other's hand.

I new it was love at first sight
The feeling was so strong
How I missed him when apart
For him, so much did I long.

Every hour and every minute counted
When together we would be
Our first kiss I never doubted,
Together we must forever be.

We have been married now a while
And every day he makes me smile.
I sometimes wonder if he really knows
Just how much our love grows.

No need for flowers and things
Just being himself, my heart sings
I cherish the day I first met him
Without his love, I would be nothing.

So you see, the tide goes out,
Ripples of water float away
But when the tide comes in again
Our love is here to stay.

J P Dawe

You Showed Me Love

When it was just me,
A person on my own,
My life, I thought, was good, OK?
I was never lonely, just alone.

I could do whatever I wanted.
Go anywhere I wanted to.
Never thought I was being selfish.
But then - oh then! I met you!

Suddenly like a door being opened,
I saw my life before me.
But a different life, a life of love.
It was as if you'd turned a key and set me free.

Now just the touch of your hand upon me
Set my nerve ends alive with fire.
And how can one look from you
Cause my resistance to crumble with desire?

When you take me in your arms
And I surrender to your kiss,
I no longer want to be alone,
Because you - yes you, have shown me something I will miss.

Never has life meant so much to me
Since you appeared like a ray of sun.
You brought love into my staid and empty world
And now my life, thanks to you, has just begun.

Sue Davan

FIRST SIGHT LOVE

I was peeling potatoes when we first met
And I fell in love at first sight.
The world stood still as our glances met
And I knew I had found Mr Right.
Two ordinary people at camp for a week,
Whose lives were miles apart
Yet a miracle happened, that wonderful day
When love started up in our heart.
With the man of my dreams I was happy all day
And we laughed at the silliest things
And talked about our innermost dreams
Even families and weddings and rings
But the golden days had to come to an end
As the real world intruded once more
There was nothing final in our farewells
For our love was forever, we were sure.
What a magical world, what fun we had
As we planned our future life
Till that happy day when we said our vows
and at last I became a wife.
What a happy life, what memories
As the years went flying past.
Although we aged, our love stayed young
Romantic and bound to last.
And that man loved me for forty-six years
And told me so every day
His love was good and strong and true
Till the day he passed away.
I still get a thrill when I recall
How we met that wonderful day
And I won't be sad, but just thank God
That love will find a way.

June Davies

ONLY IMAGINING

If I close my eyes, I can imagine you're here,
Very close, very near.
I can almost touch you, feel your skin,
I want to surrender,
Give up, give in.
You whisper to me as I lay in bed,
Lips caress me with a velvet touch
Of this moment I've dreamed so much.
I feel your breath as a kiss I steal,
I'm only imagining, but it seems so real
And though it's only a dream this time,
One day soon, you will be mine.

Deanna L Dixon

FORBIDDEN LOVE

A carefree young girl of sixteen, that was me
Dancing, fun, was all the future I could see
Boyfriends came and went, none to touch my heart
Providing light romance they played their part
And then unbidden my girlish heart was taken
Brown eyes, dark curly hair, my love did awaken
The gentle touch of his hands on mine
Kisses sweet and gentle, a love so divine
A stranger who quickly became so close and dear
Someone I wanted forever to hold me safe and near
He said that we must marry, we should be together
Such a deep and passionate love was forever
Marriage, and not a career, was to me a new concept
One that at first I did not want to accept
The Army took him many miles away
I was to meet with him again on the Sunday
During the days without him everything became clear
Why give up a wonderful life for a career
I would tell him how much I wanted to be his wife
I knew that together we would have a wonderful life
But unknown to me my father had another plan
On my love was put a cruel and sudden ban
No chance for explanations or goodbyes at all
My love never heard the sobs, or saw the tears fall
That girl has since been a mother and dutiful wife
Now she is old and nears the end of her life
But even now she can feel the despairing pain
The heartbreak of the girl overwhelms her again
That first and painful love never had its chance
But in her memory it is captured as a wonderful romance.

Margaret Meagher

RECOGNITION

I knew I loved you long before we met this time around.
A deep chasm filled up with grace.
You appeared in my life and my soul let out an exquisite sound.
I looked deep into your eyes, set in a different face.
But oh! I knew you from the very beginning.
A knowing that our chance meeting was planned.
But this time we will walk the path singing.
And create our heaven, side by side, on this land.

Marilyn Norton-Cahane

Love

The 14th of February, it's Valentine's Day,
It's time for Cupid to come out to play.
Armed with his bow and ready with his dart,
Aiming at random for an unsuspecting heart.
You don't know where they come from, they're fired from above,
And before you know it, you've fallen in love.
This man of your dreams, you'll want to spend your life
And be his all-time lover and a very caring wife.
He may be short and dumpy, he may be old and grey,
But to you it doesn't matter, you'll love him anyway.
His faults they are plenty and they say that love is blind,
So you'll only see his good points through the windows of your mind.
Through rose-coloured glasses, you'll see a loving man,
You'll always make him happy and do the best you can.
When Valentine's is over and the norm is back in play,
You wish that all that romance would happen every day.
So you will do your utmost to keep this day alive,
But don't you get disheartened, if romance takes a dive.
Just come back to Earth and get your head out of the stars,
'Cause women are from Venus, but men, they come from Mars.

Neata Todd

VALENTINE

Will you be my Valentine
And make my dreams come true?
Will you love me always
And keep me just for you?

Can I count upon you
To hold me when I cry?
Will you be my soul mate
Until the day I die?

Shall we laugh together,
When things do not go right
And make the days of pleasure
A star to crown the night?

Duchess Newman

WITHOUT A DOUBT

Know, without a doubt
How much you mean to me,
Your warmth in every little act
Is plain as plain to see.

You've given me a wondrous gift -
The chance to be myself,
This is a treasure as precious
As life itself.

In every single moment,
This gift will ever be mine,
Given freely and unselfishly,
No rod, or hook, or line.

Our dance and play at life
Is a fantastic place to be
And I pray it may continue thus
Into eternity.

Jeanette James

SEPTEMBER LOVE

It was late in the holiday season,
    On a wet September day:
It seemed for no particular reason
    That an angel came my way.

There were pearls in your eyes, pearls on your skin.
    You smiled: I asked you to stay.
And that's when I knew that Cupid would win,
    That Cupid would have his say.

Remember how we walked with rain-soaked feet,
    Caressed by the wind and spray,
Through the pearl-decked grass and the fields of wheat
    And you were a nymph at play?

Remember that kiss, that very first kiss
    On the rainbow-tinted clay?
And there in the rain was where I found bliss
    And our love was born that day.

F G Ward

LIKE AND UNLIKE

My love is like this lovely rose,
All fresh and damp with dew,
Started like a bud, then bloomed
And just grew and grew and grew.
But unlike this lovely rose,
It won't die and fade away,
My love for you, June darling,
Is here to forever stay.

E D Bowen

LOVE IS A SCARLET ROSE

(For Margaret)

Most lovers send a Valentine card, to show the way they feel,
Concerning the person who's in receipt, it proves their love is real.
But the verses written on such a card are those of someone other
And not the words from deep within, the words of their true lover.

Not everyone can pen a verse, or speak with all their heart,
That's why some many unions fail, or never get past start.
But my true love is not so blind, so something else she chose
On Valentine's Day to show her love, she sent a scarlet rose.

Garry Knowles

The Abyss

Upon the abyss
As I wait for your kiss,
How I hope that you're not just a dream.
For so often I've found,
Though feet firm on the ground,
Sometimes life is just not what it seems.

When I look in your eyes,
It will be no surprise,
That I see the great love that you give.
Your embrace will be warm,
You will do me no harm
And together so happy we'll live.

I've waited this long
For your friendship so strong,
Always hoped for this day to arrive,
When just out of the blue
My true love would be you
And within the abyss we would dive.

There together in life
We will meet all its strife,
So surrounded by love truly rare.
And yet just as I feared,
You have now disappeared,
For you're only my lover of air.

J A Brown

LOVERS

I want to captivate your sweet pulsating heart,
Kiss your luscious lips and make them part,
Caress your inner being, your soul of fire,
You are my true love, my heart's desire,
Wrap your arms around my body that is yearning,
Let's teach each other how to love forever,
We will have so much pleasure learning.

Dawn Maureen Kingsbury

A Recipe For Love

If music be the food of love
Then I hear angels up above
Singing softly whilst we dine
To soothe this appetite of mine.
Oh, how sweet the song they sing,
I will not want for anything.

John Walton

FOR AULD LANG SYNE

To send a Valentine when old
Would be presumptuous, so I'm told,
Even so I'll make so bold.
I hope it causes no distress
As who it's from, you try to guess!
Your approbation, that's my wish,
When on this card you see a kiss.
On these few words you can depend,
I'll cherish till journey's end
Thoughts of you, my childhood friend.

G Nicklin

VALENTINE'S DAY 1992

At Croydon East this special day
Commuters clutch their little spray
Of yellow freesias, roses red,
Better than a card instead.

Undying words of tender love
(Bunnikins hugs Turtledove)
Messages in tabloids - fun
(Cuddletoes loves Honeybun)

Everyone's in romance
From John O'Groats to Penzance
Alas for some there is no cure
Hopeless cases - that's for sure.

Steve Glason

LOVE IS . . .

Love is the beating of two hearts as one,
All thought of being alone now gone,
Love is wanting to be together,
Walking on air, feeling light as a feather.

Love is the joining of two minds as one,
Laughing together enjoying the same fun,
Love is to give each other much pleasure
Knowing your love will last forever.

Love is a lifetime of joy and caring,
Being selfless and kind and always sharing.
Giving each other your heart in full measure
Which will make each day another to treasure.

Jean M Wood

To A Special Man

(Dedicated to my husband Bill)

At times this life is tough and horrid,
Made worse by selfish, greedy people,
You always try to keep the peace,
And protect me from the human race.

There's trials and tears along the way,
Despite all these, your love will stay,
Sometimes the words are cruel and hurt goes deep,
These nights you lie awake, for you no sleep.

They say you can hurt the one you love most
And this can end with you counting the cost,
Two people who cannot live in harmony,
A life apart, a terrible tragedy.

Take heart my very special man,
This isn't the way for us, and if you can,
Forgive my very trying tongue,
Bear with my foibles for I'm not so young.

No words can describe how you care,
Only being here in the life we share,
The world could only be a better place,
If there were more of you to fill the space.

Elizabeth Hiddleston

To Aileen, From Afar

I look at you and I see a butterfly,
so delicate, so fragile and shy;
but not any old butterfly is it I see,
no strutting Peacock nor Painted Lady be.

No brash Red Admiral nor Common Blue,
no punk Purple Hairstreak or Swallowtail you;
no Skipper that flits on the wind like a kite,
nor Venus as seen in the Marbled White.

Your beauty is something that comes from within,
a loveliness deeper than flesh or than skin.
To me there is only one you could be,
the subtle and graceful Fritillary.

Graham Hillson

My Love

It's Valentine's Day
And I'd just like to say
To my husband Shaun,
Who I love very much,
He's gentle and kind
And always on my mind,
He's my best friend
And always there to lend a hand.
We've been together nine whole years
And my Shaun is such a dear.
Sometimes we quarrel and have our say,
But then we make up in our own special way.
It's Valentine's Day
Hip hip hooray.

B J Nortcliffe-Sills

Who?

Who has a double chin?
Who's not exactly thin?
Who can't put his shoulders back?
Whose hair is no longer black?
Who loves you in these latter years?
Who comforts you in time of tears?
Who knows your tales of days of yore?
Who's heard all your jokes before?
Who's here now passion's nearly fled?
Who said it's love that's come instead?
Who's made you a lifelong study?
Who's tailored just to be your buddy?
Who shuts the cat in every night?
Who makes the tea at dawn's first light?
Who washes shirts and also pants?
Who grows the runner beans from plants?
Who said now more folks will split up?
Who cries marriage is a fit-up?
Who cares if we're out of fashion?
Who said patience now, not passion?
Who said two can live cheap as one?
Who gave your father that shotgun?
Who sported suede with yellow tie?
Whose skirts were really rather high?
Who? Why, simply me and you.

D M Pentlow